THE TRASHY ADVENTURES
OF MILES & HIS NANA

Inspired by my grandson Miles

A special thank you to my awesome son and wonderful husband, without whom this book would never have come to fruition. And of course, an extra special thank you to Natalie for all her hard work in bringing my story to life with her beautiful illustrations. It was a family affair and a labor of love.

Copyright © 2020 By Nancy Samuels
Illustration Copyright © 2020 Illustrated By Natalie Khelif

Written by Nancy Samuels
Illustrated by Natalie Khelif
Design by Elon Khelif
All illustrations were rendered in pen and ink and watercolors.

All rights reserved. No part of this book may be reproduced in any form without the express written permission of the author and/or illustrator.

ISBN: 978-0-578-66104-9

Once upon a time, there was a boy named Miles and his Nana named, well…Nana.

They loved each other very very much.

And getting messy with finger paints,

And in the summer time,

they loved to cool off in the swimming pool.

As they walked, Nana explained some people just don't understand if they throw trash all over the place, the world won't be as beautiful.

So on their next walk, they brought a **big** paper bag and started to pick up the **trash** they saw on the ground.

THERE WAS A LOT OF IT!

As they strolled along they did their very **best** to pick up every piece of **trash** they saw.

When their bag was full and they were heading home, they realized if every person picked up just one piece of trash everyday, their neighborhood and the whole world wouldn't have any trash, and the world would be even more beautiful!

So Miles decided he would pick up
trash on all his walks
to help make the **world** a better place.

THE END

Made in the USA
Middletown, DE
03 April 2020